I0828191

THIS BOOK BELONGS TO:

WELCOME TO NEVADA

Dedicated to all the explorers.

ISBN 978-1-970416-02-2

www.joeysavestheday.com

Mimi Books™ Publishing

A Mimi Book

Nevada got its name from the Spanish word "nevada," which means "snow-covered." Early explorers used the word to describe the tall, snowy mountains in the region, especially the Sierra Nevada. Even though much of the state is desert, those snowy peaks inspired the name.

Carson Range in Western Nevada

Nevada has a long history that begins with Native American nations who lived among its deserts, mountains, and valleys for thousands of years. Tribes such as the Paiute, Shoshone, and Washoe built strong communities across the region. In the 1800s, explorers and traders arrived, followed later by settlers drawn to the area's mining opportunities.

Nevada was the thirty-sixth state to join the Union. It officially became a state on October 31, 1864.

Nevada is located in the western United States. It is bordered by California, Oregon, Idaho, Utah, and Arizona.

Carson City is the capital of Nevada.
It officially became the capital in 1864.

Carson City, Nevada, has an estimated population of about 58,600 people.

Carson City
STATE CAPITAL

NEVADA

Nevada is the seventh largest state in the United States by area.

There are approximately 3,282,000 people residing in the state of Nevada.

Kit Carson, a well-known frontiersman and explorer of the American West, is remembered in Nevada through the state's capital city, Carson City, which was named in his honor.

Nevada is famous for its tasty shrimp cocktail! This chilly, yummy treat became popular in early Las Vegas, where restaurants served it in tall glasses filled with zesty sauce. Today, people all over Nevada enjoy shrimp cocktail at buffets, celebrations, and special events.

celebrate

NEVADA

There are 16 counties in Nevada and 1 independent city.

Here is a list of those sixteen counties:

Churchill	Esmeralda	Lincoln	Pershing
Clark	Eureka	Lyon	Storey
Douglas	Humboldt	Mineral	Washoe
Elko	Lander	Nye	White Pine

City: Carson

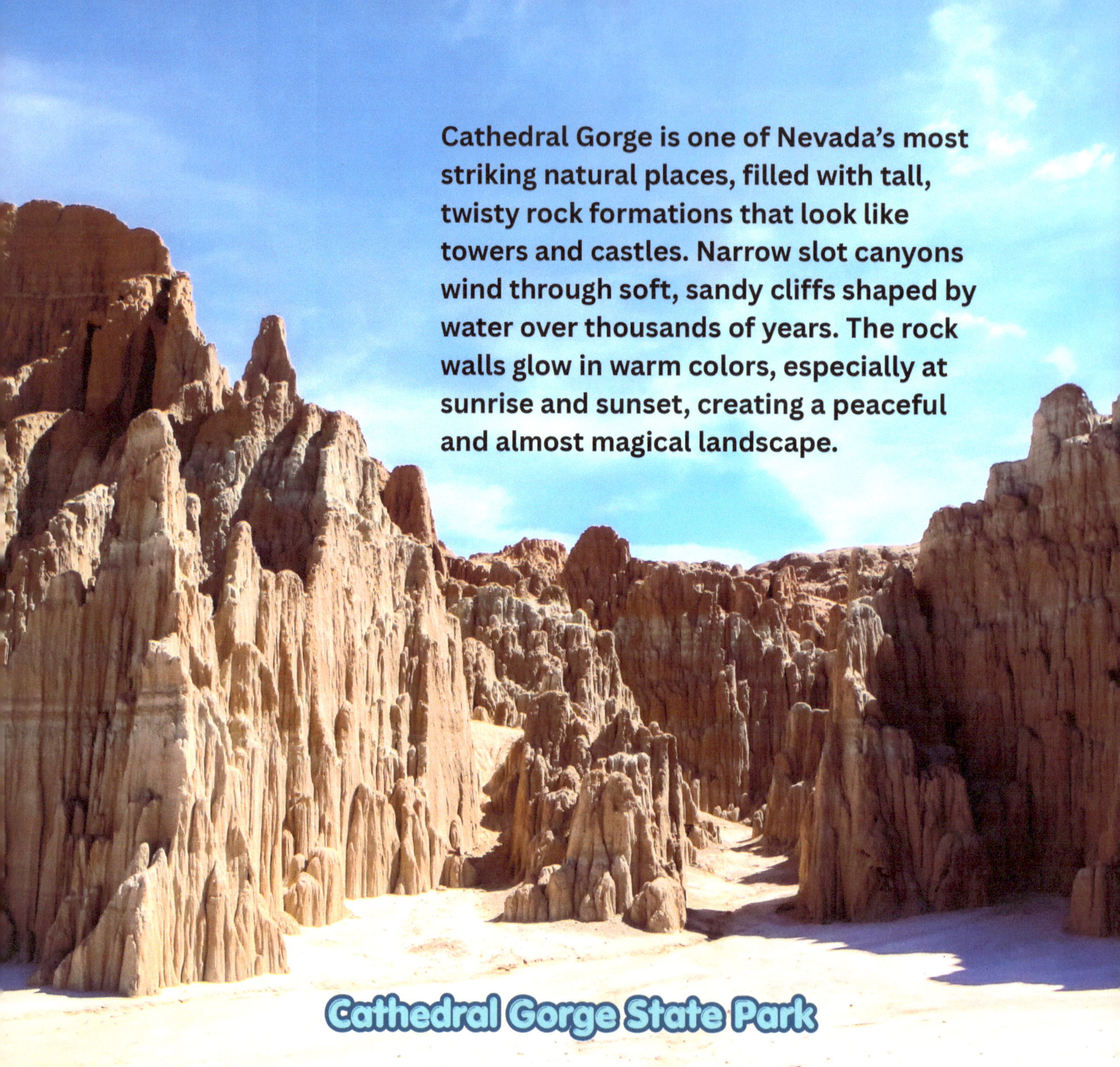

Cathedral Gorge is one of Nevada's most striking natural places, filled with tall, twisty rock formations that look like towers and castles. Narrow slot canyons wind through soft, sandy cliffs shaped by water over thousands of years. The rock walls glow in warm colors, especially at sunrise and sunset, creating a peaceful and almost magical landscape.

Cathedral Gorge State Park

One of the most important moments in Nevada's history is the discovery of the Comstock Lode in 1859. This massive silver deposit, found near present-day Virginia City, became one of the richest mineral strikes in American history. The discovery brought thousands of miners and families to the region, helping small camps grow into busy towns and turning Nevada into a major center for mining and industry.

ACHIEVMENT

The Hoover Dam is a historic landmark that sits on the border of Nevada and Arizona, holding back the mighty Colorado River to form Lake Mead. Built during the 1930s, this massive concrete structure is one of America's most famous engineering achievements!

The Nevada state bird is the Mountain Bluebird. It was chosen as the state bird in 1967.

The official state flower of Nevada is the Sagebrush. It was chosen as the state flower in 1917.

A couple of Nevada's nicknames include the Silver State and the Battle Born State.

ST8

ST8

Nevada's state motto is "All for Our Country." It was adopted in 1866.

What "All for Our Country" Means:

- The motto shows that Nevada values loyalty and service to the United States.
- It reflects the state's strong support for the country, especially during the Civil War era, when Nevada became a state.

Put together, the motto is saying:
Nevada believes in working together, supporting the nation, and standing strong for the good of the country.

The abbreviation for Nevada is NV.

Nevada's state flag was
officially adopted in 1929.
BATTLE BORN
NEVADA

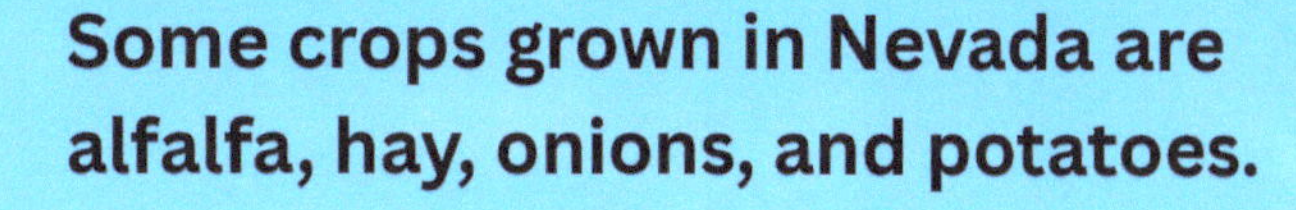

Some crops grown in Nevada are alfalfa, hay, onions, and potatoes.

Some animals that live in Nevada are mule deer, coyotes, jackrabbits, desert bighorn sheep, and roadrunners.

Nevada experiences a wide range of temperatures throughout the year. The hottest temperature ever recorded in the state was 125 degrees Fahrenheit, measured in Laughlin on June 29, 1994. In contrast, the coldest temperature documented was −50 degrees Fahrenheit, recorded in San Jacinto on January 8, 1937.

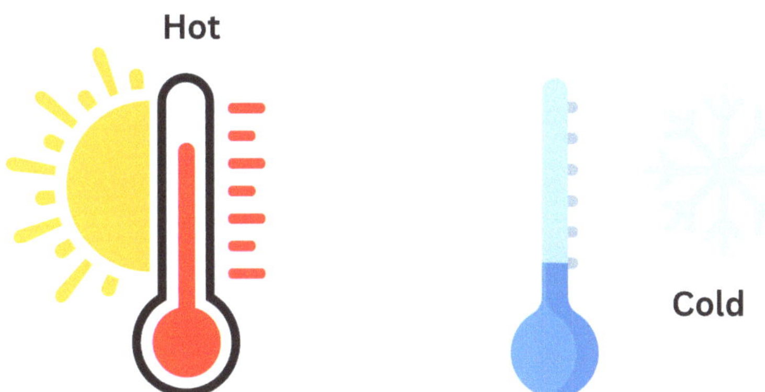

The Las Vegas Springs Preserve in Las Vegas is a wonderful place to explore, with animals from all around the world. Kids can see desert tortoises, foxes, lizards, birds of prey, and playful mammals, along with colorful birds and reptiles.

Robert Goddard was a famous rocket scientist who worked in Nevada while testing some of the world's first modern rockets. His experiments helped people learn how rockets could travel higher and faster. People remember him for his groundbreaking ideas and for helping launch the age of space exploration.

The largest airport in Nevada is Harry Reid International Airport, located in Las Vegas. It sits at 5757 Wayne Newton Boulevard and serves as the main travel hub for people flying in and out of Nevada. This airport connects travelers to cities all across the country and to destinations around the world, making it one of the busiest and most important airports in the western United States.

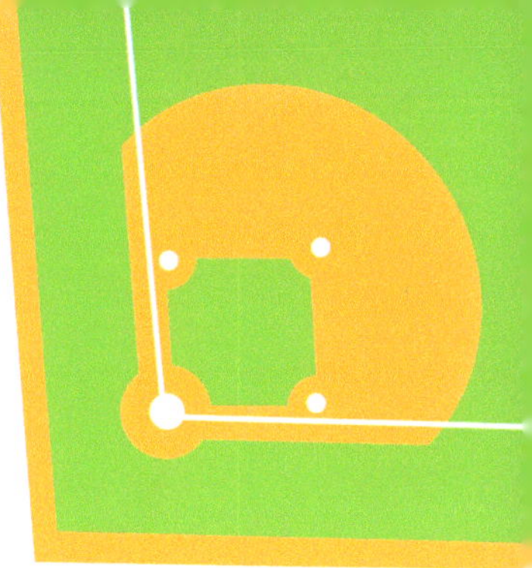

The Las Vegas Aviators are a professional baseball team based in Las Vegas, one of Nevada's most exciting and fast-growing cities. They play their home games at Las Vegas Ballpark, a bright and modern stadium known for its lively atmosphere, stunning desert views, and fan-friendly design. The Aviators have welcomed many talented players over the years, giving them a place to grow their skills and make their mark in the world of baseball.

FOOTBALL

The Las Vegas Raiders are a major professional football team with a huge fan base all across Nevada, where many families cheer for them every season. The team plays its home games at Allegiant Stadium in Las Vegas, a loud and energetic stadium filled with fans wearing silver and black.

Natural Beauty

The single-leaf pinyon is Nevada's state tree. It's known for its sturdy branches, short needles, and the tasty pine nuts it produces, which have been important to the region for generations. The single-leaf pinyon was officially adopted as the state tree in 1953, and its strength and resilience make it a proud symbol of Nevada's natural beauty.

The Lahontan cutthroat trout is Nevada's state fish. It's a sleek, spotted trout known for its shimmering colors and the bright red-orange streaks along its sides. The Lahontan cutthroat trout was officially adopted as the state fish in 1981, and it is an important symbol of Nevada's rivers, lakes, and desert waterways.

Can you name these?

I hope you enjoyed learning about Nevada.

To explore fun facts about the other 49 states, visit my website at www.joeysavestheday.com. You'll also find a wide variety of homeschool resources to support joyful learning at home. If you enjoyed this book, I would be grateful if you left a review. Your feedback truly helps. Thank you for your support!

Check out these other interesting books in the 50 States Fact Books Series!

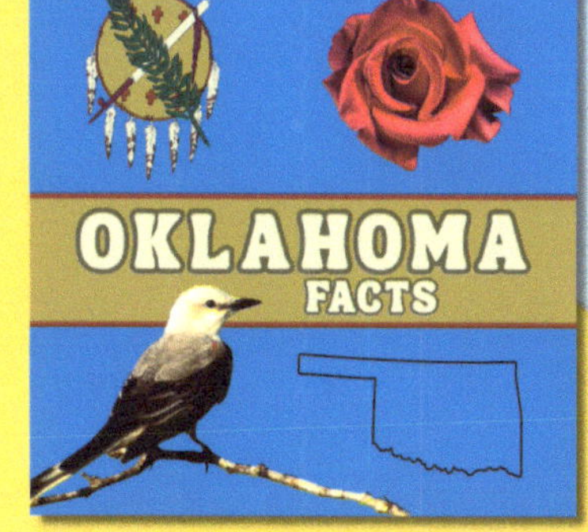

www.mimibooks.com